Colonial America
Reference Library
Cumulative Index

Colonial America
Reference Library
Cumulative Index

Cumulates Indexes For:

Colonial America: Almanac
Colonial America: Biographies
Colonial America: Primary Sources

Julie Carnagie,
Index Coordinator

U·X·L®

AN IMPRINT OF THE GALE GROUP

DETROIT · NEW YORK · SAN FRANCISCO
LONDON · BOSTON · WOODBRIDGE, CT

Julie L. Carnagie, *Index Coordinator*

Printed in the United States of America

10 9 8 7 6 5 4 3 2 1

Cumulative Index

A = Colonial America: Almanac
B = Colonial America: Biographies
PS = Colonial America: Primary Sources

A

Abolitionism
 A *1:* 141, 174
 B *2:* 302, 378, 380, 382
 PS 185, 190
Academy and College of
  Philadelphia
 A *2:* 339
 PS 288-89
Acosta, Jose de
 A *2:* 375
Adams, Abigail Smith
 A *2:* 280
 PS 296, 296 (ill.)
Adams, John
 A *1:* 183
 PS **285-97**, 293 (ill.)
Adams, John Quincy
 PS 297
Addison, Joseph
 A *2:* 365
Adena
 A *1:* 9
African American oral tradition
 A *2:* 363

African religions
 A *2:* 296
Africans in America
 B *1:* 155
Agriculture
 A *1:* 190-91, 193, 199
Alarcón, Hernando de
 A *1:* 48
 B *1:* 71
Albany Congress
 A *1:* 78
Alden, John
 B *1:* 18-19
Alexander, James
 PS 160-61
Alexander VI
 PS 159
Algonquins
 A *1:* 21, 66, 68; *2:* 302
 B *1:* 53-54, 101-02, 105
 PS 106
Allston, Washington
 B *2:* 308
Alston, Charles
 B *1:* 57

Bold type indicates set title, main entries, and their page numbers

Italic type indicates volume numbers

Illustrations are marked by (ill.).

Alvarado, Hernando de
  A *1:* 48
  B *1:* 72
Amadas, Philip
  A *1:* 80
  PS 52
American Civil War
  B *1:* 38, 117
American Company
  A *2:* 366
American Lutheran Church
  B *2:* 225
American Philosophical Society
  B *1:* 126
American Revolution
  A *1:* 118, 138; *2:* 404
  B *1:* 7; *2:* 249
  PS 143
Amherst, Jeffrey
  B *1:* 86; *2:* 267, 269-70
Anabaptists
  PS 222
Anasazi
  A *1:* 10
Anderson, Hugh
  A *2:* 363
Androboros
  A *2:* 365
Andros, Edmund
  A *1:* 98, 105, 169-70, 169 (ill.)
  B *1:* 37, 196
  PS 105, 229
The Angel of Bethesda
  B *2:* 206, 211
Anglican Church
  A *2:* 278
Anglicanism
  A *1:* 114; *2:* 278, 293, 295-96,
    298, 300, 310, 314, 316, 318
Anglicans
  A *2:* 240
Anklin, Benjamin
  B *1:* 128-29, 132
Annapolis, Maryland
  A *1:* 113; *2:* 336
Apaches
  A *1:* 51; *2:* 291, 320
  B *2:* 273-74, 277
  PS 32-33, 38
Apprenticeship
  A *1:* 200
Archaic Age
  A *1:* 5-7

Argall, Samuel
  B *2:* 262-63
Arias, Pedro
  A *1:* 41
  B *2:* 317
Arithmetica
  B *2:* 385
Ashbridge, Elizabeth
  PS 261-69
Astrology
  A *2:* 386-87
Astronomy
  A *2:* 383, 385
"The Author to Her Book"
  PS 247-48
Avavares
  B *1:* 121
Aztecs
  A *1:* 7, 10
Aztlán
  A *1:* 10

B

Backerus, Johannes
  A *2:* 329
Backus, Isaac
  A *2:* 307, 308 (ill.)
Bacon, Elizabeth
  A *1:* 136
  PS 131-43
Bacon, Francis
  B *1:* 2; *2:* 207
Bacon, Nathaniel
  A *1:* 135 (ill.), 136-38
  B *1:* 1-7, 1 (ill.), 6 (ill.), 36
  PS 134-37, 135 (ill.), 139 (ill.),
    140, 142-43
Bacon's Castle
  A *2:* 372
"Bacon's Laws"
  B *1:* 4
Bacon's Rebellion
  A *1:* 29, 137-38
  B *1:* 1-2, 5, 7, 36, 196
  PS 135-36, 142-43
Bacon, Thomas
  B *1:* 2
Bahama Channel
  A *1:* 115
Baker, Richard
  B *1:* 116

Banjo
  A *2:* 353
Baptists
  A *1:* 151; *2:* 306-07, 318
  B *2:* 368
  PS 208
Barbados
  A *1:* 116, 119
Baron, Pierre
  A *2:* 368
Bartram, John
  A *2:* 385
  B *1:* **8-12,** 8 (ill.) 57
Bartram, William
  B *1:* 10-11, 57
Batts, Thomas
  A *2:* 378
Bayard, Judith
  B *2:* 330
The Bay Psalm Book
  A *2:* 359
**"Before the Birth of One of
  Her Children"**
  B *1:* 23
  PS 246-47
Beissel, Johann Conrad
  A *2:* 316
Belknap, Ruth
  B *1:* 27
  PS 251
Benavides, Fray Alonso de
  PS 27-38
*Benjamin Franklin: A Biography
  in His Own Words*
  B *1:* 132
  PS 271-84
Bennett, Edward
  B *1:* 154
Bennett, Richard
  B *1:* 156
Beothuk
  A *1:* 12
Bering Sea Land Bridge
  A *1:* 5
Bering, Vitus
  PS 6, 6 (ill.)
Berkeley, George
  B *2:* 306
Berkeley, William
  A *1:* 133-35, 135 (ill.), 138
  B *1:* 1, 4-5, 7, 196
  PS 132-36, 132 (ill.),
    139 (ill.), 142

The Bermuda Group
  A *2:* 345
  B *2:* 307
Beverley, Robert
  A *2:* 363
  B *1:* 36
  PS 169-80
Bienville, Jean Baptiste Le Moyne,
    sieur de
  A *1:* 76-77
Bifocals
  B *1:* 131
  PS 283
Blackbeard
  A *1:* 120
  B *1:* 170, 170 (ill.)
Blair, James
  A *2:* 296
*The Bloudy Tenent of Persecution for
    Cause of Conscience*
  B *2:* 369
Bobadilla, Francisco de
  A *1:* 36
  B *1:* 66
  PS 24
Bogardus, Everardus
  A *2:* 329
Bond Castle
  A *2:* 371
Bonney, Anne
  B *1:* 172
Bonney, James
  B *1:* 172
Boston, Massachusetts
  A *2:* 211, 215, 278-79, 281
Boyle, Robert
  A *2:* 323
  B *1:* 37, 102; *2:* 210
Boylston, Zabdiel
  A *2:* 392
  PS 297
Bradford, William
  A *1:* 90, 92-93, 142-43; *2:* 358
  B *1:* **13-20,** 13 (ill.); *2:* 202, 220,
    299, 326, 367, 385
  PS 39, **77-88,** 79 (ill.), 199-200,
    279
Bradley, Richard
  B *2:* 387-88
  PS 161-62, 164
Bradstreet, Anne
  A *2:* 281, 360
  B *1:* **21-28**
  PS **241-51,** 243 (ill.)

Bradstreet, Simon
  A *2:* 281
  PS 244
Brainerd, David
  A *2:* 250
Brainerd, John
  A *2:* 250
Brattle, Thomas
  A *2:* 385
Brébeuf, Jean de
  B *1:* 134
  PS 40 (ill.), 41
Brent, John
  A *1:* 135
  B *1:* 3
  PS 133
Brent, Margaret
  A *1:* 178; *2:* 280
  B *1:* **29-34**
  PS 255
Brereton, John
  A *2:* 377
Brewster, William
  B *1:* 14
Bridges, Charles
  A *2:* 345
A Brief and True Report of the
    New Found Land of Virginia
  A *2:* 376
  PS 51-63
A Briefe Description of New-York
  A *2:* 361
A Brief Explication and Proof of the
    Philolaick Systeme
  A *2:* 386
A Brief History of the Warr with the
    Indians of New England
  A *2:* 357
A Brief Narrative of the Case
    and Tryal of John Peter
    Zenger
  B *2:* 387 88
  PS 159-67
Brigden, Zechariah
  A *2:* 386
Briggs, Henry
  A *2:* 379
Broullé, Hélène
  B *1:* 51
Broutin, François
  A *2:* 368
Browne, John
  B *1:* 109

Browne, Samuel
  B *1:* 109
Buade, Louis de
  A *1:* 68
  B *1:* 186
  PS 42
Budd, Thomas
  A *2:* 361
Bull, William
  A *1:* 118
Burgess, William
  A *2:* 347
Byles, Mather
  A *2:* 361
Bylot, Robert
  B *1:* 142
Byrd II, William
  A *2:* 218, 218 (ill.), 363, 372,
    397-98, 403, 406-07
  B *1:* **35-41**, 35 (ill.)

C

Cabeza de Vaca, Alvar Núñez
  A *1:* 39-40, 40 (ill.); *2:* 355, 355
    (ill.)
  B *1:* 69-70, 120-23; *2:* 318
Cabot, John
  A *1:* 59, 79, 102
  PS 51, 52 (ill.), 101
Cabot, Sebastian
  A *1:* 79
Cadwalader, Thomas
  A *2:* 391
Cahokia
  A *1:* 9
Cahokia Courthouse
  A *2:* 368
Calmecac
  A *2:* 326
Calvert, Cecilius
  A *1:* 113-14, 165; *2:* 293
  B *1:* 30, 34
Calvert, Charles
  B *1:* 31; *2:* 248
Calvert, George
  A *1:* 112; *2:* 293
  B *1:* 31
  PS 99
Calvert, Leonard
  A *1:* 114
  B *1:* 32-33

Calvinism
   B *1:* 192, 194, 196
Calvinists
   B *1:* 169; *2:* 227
   PS 108
Calvin, John
   A *2:* 298, 299 (ill.), 304, 309-10,
      351
   B *1:* 193
Cambridge Agreement
   A *1:* 95
   B *2:* 375
   PS 221
Cambridge, Massachusetts
   A *2:* 336
Campanius, John
   A *2:* 309
Campbell, Colin
   A *2:* 372
Campbell, John
   A *1:* 209
Cape Fear River
   A *1:* 116
Cárdenas, Garcia Lopez de
   B *1:* 72
A Careful and Strict Enquiry Into . . .
      Freedom of Will
   B *1:* 99
Carolinas
   A *1:* 17-18, 115-16,
      116 (ill.), 118
Cartier, Jacques
   A *1:* 58-61, 60 (ill.)
   B *1:* **42-47**, 42 (ill.), 43 (ill.)
Carver, John
   A *1:* 91-92
   B *1:* 13, 16
Casor, John
   B *1:* 158
   PS 80-81
Casteñeda, Pedro de
   A *1:* 47; *2:* 355
   B *1:* 119, 122
Castillo, Alonzo de
   A *1:* 39
   B *1:* 121
Castillo de San Marcos
   A *2:* 367
Catesby, Mark
   B *1:* 10
Catherine of Aragon
   A *1:* 89; *2:* 294-95
   PS 77-78

Catholic Church
   A *2:* 288-89, 300
Catholicism
   A *2:* 288, 291, 293, 295,
      298, 308
   B *1:* 14
Cato's Letters
   A *2:* 365
   PS 160
Cayugas
   A *1:* 21-22
   B *1:* 84
Chabot, Philippe de
   A *1:* 57
   B *2:* 354
Champlain, Samuel de
   A *1:* 63-64, 64 (ill.), 160; *2:* 321,
      356, 378, 378 (ill.)
   B *1:* **48-54**, 48 (ill.), 50 (ill.);
      2: 324
   PS 41
A Character of the Province
      of Mary-land
   A *2:* 363
Charlesfort
   A *1:* 115
Charles I
   A *1:* 95, 97, 115, 151; *2:* 293
   B *1:* 14, 22, 26; *2:* 318, 365,
      373-74
   PS 207, 220, 224, 244
Charles II
   A *1:* 101, 105, 192; *2:* 404
   B *1:* 30; *2:* 247, 333
   PS 90 (ill.), 105, 112
Charleston, South Carolina
   A *1:* 116; *2:* 211, 341
Charles Town
   A *1:* 117-18
Charlevoix, Pierre François
      Xavier de
   A *2:* 356
Chartier de la Lotbiniére,
      René-Louis
   A *2:* 356
Cheever, Ezekiel
   A *2:* 332
   PS **145-58**
Cherokees
   A *1:* 4, 25; *2:* 257, 323
Chesapeake Bay
   A *1:* 113
Chickasaws
   A *1:* 18, 20

Chirikov, Aleksey
  PS 6
Choctaws
  A *1:* 18
The Christian Commonwealth
  B *1:* 105
"Christopher Columbus Reports to Ferdinand and Isabella"
  PS 15-26
A Chronological History of New-England
  A *2:* 358
Church of England
  A *1:* 99, 112
Circulation of air masses
  B *1:* 130
Claiborne Rebellion
  A *1:* 114
  B *1:* 33
Claiborne, William
  A *1:* 114
  B *1:* 33, 33 (ill.)
Clarke, John
  B *1:* 90
Clark, William
  B *1:* 12
Clayton, John
  A *2:* 385
  B *1:* 10
Clement, Augustine
  A *2:* 344
Clement, Samuel
  A *2:* 344
Clopton, Thomasine
  B *2:* 372
  PS 220
Clyfton, Richard
  B *1:* 14
Cochiti Pueblo
  A *1:* 6
Coddington, William
  A *1:* 101
Coke, Edward
  B *2:* 363
Colbert, Jean-Baptiste
  A *2:* 340
Colden, Cadwallader
  A *2:* 361, 380, 385
  B *1:* 10, 55, 56 (ill.), 58
Colden, Jane
  A *2:* 380
  B *1:* 10, 55-58

Coligny, Gaspar de Châtillon, comte de
  A *1:* 62
College of William and Mary
  A *2:* 323, 338
  B *1:* 102
  PS 287
Collinson, Peter
  A *2:* 388
  B *1:* 8, 10-11, 57
Colonial America, map of
  A *1:* 187 (ill.)
Colonists
  PS 10 (ill.)
Columbus, Bartholomew
  A *1:* 36
  B *1:* 63, 66
  PS 24
Columbus, Christopher
  A *1:* 1, 13-14, 32-36, 33 (ill.), 34 (ill.), 44; *2:* 288
  B *1:* **59-67**, 59 (ill.), 61 (ill); *2:* 330
  PS 3, **15-26**, 17 (ill.), 21 (ill.), 37
Columbus, Diego
  A *1:* 36
  B *1:* 60, 66
  PS 24
Columbus, Fernando
  A *1:* 34
  B *1:* 60
Comanches
  A *2:* 320
"The Coming of the First White Man"
  PS 3-13, 18
Company of Comedians
  A *2:* 366
Company of the Indies
  A *1:* 76
The Compleat Housewife
  A *2:* 390
Congregationalism
  A *2:* 317-18
  B *2:* 299
Congregationalists
  B *2:* 373
Connecticut
  A *1:* 99-100, 164, 209; *2:* 212, 250, 324, 339
Conquistadors
  B *1:* 69
The Conscious Lovers
  A *2:* 366

Conservation of charge
  B *1:* 129
Considerations on the Keeping
    of Negroes
  B *2:* 381
Constantine XI
  B *2:* 310
Cook, Ebenezer
  A *2:* 364
Cooper, Anthony Ashley
  A *1:* 116
Cooper, Susannah
  A *2:* 281
Coote, Richard
  B *1:* 171, 173, 198
Copernicus, Nicholas
  A *2:* 383, 385
Copley, John Singleton
  A *2:* 347
  B *2:* 308
Coronado, Francisco Vásquez de
  A *1:* 15, 47-50, 49 (ill.); *2:* 355
  B *1:* **68-74**, 70 (ill.), 71 (ill.),
    119, 125; *2:* 274
  PS 28, 29 (ill.)
Cortés, Hernán
  A *1:* 37
  B *1:* 69
  PS 27
Cosby, William
  A *1:* 175
  B *2:* 384-87
  PS 160-62
Cotton, John
  A *1:* 151-54; *2:* 276
  B *1:* 23, **75-80**, 75 (ill), 144;
    2: 207
  PS 208-09, 211, 244
Council for New England
  A *1:* 95
  B *1:* 19; *2:* 374
  PS 220
Council of Virginia
  B *1:* 35
Courcelle, Rémy de
  A *2:* 356
Couturier, Henri
  A *2:* 343
Covenant Chain
  A *1:* 22-23
Covenant of grace
  A *1:* 152; *2:* 299
  PS 195, 210

Covenant of works
  A *1:* 151
  PS 208
Coytmore, Martha
  B *2:* 377
Craddock, Matthew
  B *1:* 108
Creeks
  A *1:* 17-18
Crèvecouer, J. Hector St. John
  A *2:* 283
Croghan, George
  B *1:* **81-87**, 81 (ill.), 163
Cromwell, Oliver
  B *1:* 26
Cross, Martha
  A *2:* 272
Crusades
  A *1:* 31
  PS 15
Cuentos
  A *2:* 355
Cullen, Susan
  B *1:* 117
Cushman, Robert
  A *1:* 94

D

Daganowedah
  A *1:* 21-22
Dale, Thomas
  B *2:* 263-64, 287
D'Alibard
  B *1:* 129
Dame schools
  PS 285
Danckaerts, Jasper
  A *2:* 338
  B *2:* 347, 349
  PS 288
The Daniel Catcher
  A *2:* 362
Darby, William
  A *2:* 365
Dare, Virginia
  PS 63
Dartmouth College
  A *2:* 324
Davenport, James
  B *2:* 361
Davenport, John
  A *1:* 100

Davenport, Rachel
  A *2:* 274
Day, Dorothy
  B *1:* 14
The Day of Doom
  B *2:* 337
  PS 243
De Harana, Diego
  B *1:* 62
De Lancey, James
  B *2:* 385-87
  PS 160-63, 165, 167
Delaware Prophet
  B *2:* 269
Delawares
  A *1:* 19, 23, 164, 181; *2:* 212, 277
  B *1:* 86, 141; *2:* 268, 271
  PS 4
De La Warr, Thomas West
  A *1:* 87
  PS 74
Delisle, Guillaume
  A *2:* 379
Dellius, Godfriedus
  A *2:* 324
*A Description of the New
    Netherland*
  A *2:* 361
Deshon, Moses
  A *2:* 349
**The Diary and Autobiography of
    John Adams**
  PS 285-97
Diary Entries of Samuel Sewall
  PS 145-58
Díaz, Melchor
  A *1:* 48
  B *1:* 71-72
Dinwiddie, Robert
  B *1:* 102
Diseases, Native American
  A *1:* 26 (ill.)
Distilleries
  A *1:* 195
Doctors, colonial
  A *2:* 391 (ill.)
Doeg
  A *1:* 135
  B *1:* 3
  PS 133
Dominion of New England
  A *1:* 169-70
  B *1:* 196
  PS 229

Donck, Junker van der
  B *2:* 331
Dongan, Thomas
  B *1:* 193-94
Donnacona
  A *1:* 59, 61
  B *1:* 43, 46
Douglas, David
  A *2:* 364
Douglass, Frederick
  B *1:* 117
Douglass, William
  A *2:* 362, 392-93
Drake, Francis
  A *1:* 81, 115
  PS 53
Drayton Hall
  A *2:* 373
Drisius, Samuel
  A *2:* 322
Du Bartas, Guillaume de Salluste
  B *1:* 25
Dudley, Thomas
  B *1:* 22
  PS 244
Duke, Elizabeth
  B *1:* 2
"Dunkers"
  A *2:* 316
Duodecennium Luctuosum
  A *2:* 358
Du Pont, François Gravé
  A *1:* 63
  B *1:* 49
Duston, Hannah
  A *2:* 282
  B *2:* 294
Duston, Thomas
  B *2:* 294
Dutch
  A *1:* 163, 181; *2:* 213 (ill.)
Dutch colonial houses
  A *2:* 371
Dutch Reformed Church
  A *2:* 310
Dutch West India Company
  A *1:* 102-04, 163; *2:* 310-11,
    322, 328, 340
  B *1:* 138, 194; *2:* 330-31, 351
  PS 101-04, 106, 115
Dutton, John
  A *2:* 396
Duyckinck, Gerardus
  A *2:* 344

Duyckinck, Gerrit
  A *2:* 344
Duyckinck III, Evert
  A *2:* 343-44
Dyer, Mary
  A *2:* 278, 278 (ill.)
  B *1:* **88-93**, 88 (ill.), 91 (ill.),
    111, 150; *2:* 368
Dyer, William
  B *1:* 89

E

Eames, Henry
  A *2:* 349
*Early Part Life of the Life of
    Elizabeth Ashbridge*
  PS 264, 268
"The Earth Speaks to Its
    Cultivator"
  A *2:* 362
East India Company
  B *1:* 170
Easton, John
  PS **119-30**
Eaton, Theophilus
  A *1:* 100
Edict of Nantes
  B *1:* 195
Edwards, Jonathan
  A *2:* 303 (ill.), 304, 317, 333
  B *1:* **94-100**, 94 (ill.); *2:* 360
Edwards, Sarah Piedmont
  A *2:* 277
  B *1:* 95-96
Edward III
  B *1:* 30
Electrical condenser
  B *1:* 128
Electricity
  B *1:* 126, 128-31
  PS 272, 281-82
Eliot, John
  A *2:* 302, 316, 341
  B *1:* **101-06**, 101 (ill.), 104 (ill.)
  PS 122, 122 (ill.)
Elizabeth I
  A *1:* 62, 80, 89
  B *1:* 26; *2:* 373-74
  PS 52, 78
Ellis, Sarah
  B *2:* 379

Emmes, Thomas
  A *2:* 347
Encomienda
  A *2:* 214-16
Endecott, John
  A *1:* 94, 96, 143-44; *2:* 278
  B *1:* 90-92, **107-12**, 107 (ill.);
    2: 222
  PS 203, 220-21, 224
England
  PS 85
English civil war
  A *1:* 115; *2:* 293, 404
Enriquez, Beatriz
  A *1:* 34
  B *1:* 60
Enstone, Edward
  A *2:* 353
Entertainment for a Winter's Evening
  A *2:* 361
Equiano, Olaudah
  B *1:* **113-18**, 113 (ill.); *2:* 380
  PS 183, 188-89, 189 (ill.)
Eries
  A *1:* 17
Eriksson, Leif
  A *1:* 12-13
  PS 12
Erik the Red
  A *1:* 12-13, 13 (ill.)
  B *2:* 351
  PS 12
Estevanico
  A *1:* 39-40, 46-47
  B *1:* 69, **119-25**, 119 (ill.)
Estrada, Beatriz de
  A *1:* 49
  B *1:* 69
Examination Act
  A *2:* 306
**Excerpt From the Trial of Anne
    Hutchinson**
  PS **207-16**
Excise taxes
  A *1:* 183

F

Fairbanks house
  A *2:* 370
*A Faithful Narrative of the
    Surprising Work of God*
  B *1:* 97

Fallam, Robert
  A *2:* 378
Faneuil, Peter
  B *2:* 307, 307 (ill.)
Farfán de los Godos, Marcos
  A *2:* 364
Farming
  A *1:* 189-92, 190 (ill.); *2:* 243
Farquhar, William
  B *1:* 58
Farrer, John
  A *2:* 377
Feke, Robert
  A *2:* 347
Fell, Margaret
  A *2:* 277
Ferdinand V
  A *1:* 32-33, 35-36; *2:* 288
  B *1:* 60, 64-65
  PS 17, 17 (ill.), 23-24
Fernández de Córdoba, Francisco
  A *1:* 41
  B *2:* 317
First Amendment
  PS 167
"The First Fire"
  A *1:* 4
Fishing
  A *1:* 402 (ill.)
Fitch, Elizabeth
  B *2:* 336
Five Nations
  A *1:* 23-24
"The Flying Spider"
  A *2:* 333
  B *1:* 96
Folger, Peter
  PS 273
Formative Period
  A *1:* 5, 7-8
Forth, Mary
  B *2:* 372
  PS 220
Fort Ponchartrain
  A *1:* 24
Foster, John
  A *2:* 347, 386
Fothergill, John
  B *1:* 10
"The Founding of Jamestown"
  PS 65-76, 169
Fox, George
  A *1:* 106; *2:* 312

  B *1:* 90; *2:* 245, 247, 369, 379
  PS 89
Foxhunting
  A *2:* 407-08, 408 (ill.)
Franchise Act
  A *1:* 134, 137
  B *1:* 2-3, 5
  PS 132, 135
Franciscans
  A *1:* 51; *2:* 290, 320, 325, 351,
    355, 366
  PS 29, 39
François I
  A *1:* 56-58, 61
  B *1:* 43, 46; *2:* 352-53
Franklin, Benjamin
  A *1:* 109, 209; *2:* 339, 357,
    386-88, 389 (ill.)
  B *1:* 11, **126-32**, 126 (ill.);
    2: 206, 359-60, 383
  PS **271-84**, 272 (ill.),
    276 (ill.), 289
Franklin stove
  B *1:* 131
  PS 283
Franks, Abigail
  A *2:* 398
**"Fray Alonso de Benavides
    Reports New Mexico
    Indians Eager for
    Conversion"**
  PS 27-38
Freedom of the press
  B *2:* 384, 388
  PS 159, 166
Frelinghuysen, Theodorus
    Jacobus
  A *2:* 306, 310
French
  A *1:* 160
French and Indian War
  A *1:* 77, 162; *2:* 320
French Company of the West
  A *1:* 76
Frobisher, Martin
  A *1:* 80
  B *1:* 142
  PS 52
Fur trade
  A *1:* 191

G

Galileo
A *2:* 383, 386

Ganz, Joachim
A *2:* 376

Garden, Alexander
B *1:* 57

Geography
A *2:* 376

George, Lydia Lee
B *2:* 212

George II
A *1:* 120
B *2:* 238

George III
B *2:* 226, 228

Georgia
A *1:* 18, 164, 167, 184;
2: 233, 341

Georgian architecture
A *2:* 372-73

German Reform Church
A *2:* 312

Gibson, Elizabeth
B *1:* 108

Gilbert, Humphrey
A *1:* 80
PS 52

Giton, Judith
A *2:* 265

Glorious Revolution
A *1:* 98, 114, 170, 184; *2:* 293
PS 229

Godfrey, Thomas
A *2:* 366

God's Determinations Touching his Elect
B *2:* 336

"God's Promise to His Plantations"
B *1:* 78

Good Order Established in Pennsilvania & New-Jersey
A *2:* 361

Gookin, Daniel
A *2:* 358

Gordon, Thomas
PS 160

Gorges, Ferdinando
A *1:* 97, 144-45
B *2:* 223-24
PS 203-04, 224

Gorton, Samuel
A *1:* 101

Gosnold, Bartholomew
A *1:* 79, 88
B *2:* 312
PS 51, 67, 69, 77

Gouldsmith, Samuel
B *1:* 157

Governor's Palace
A *2:* 366, 367 (ill.)

Gower, Ann
B *1:* 108

Gracia Real de Santa Teresa de Mose
A *2:* 234
PS 191

Grajales, Francisco López De Mendoza
A *1:* 44
PS 37

Grave markers
A *2:* 348, 348 (ill.)

Great Awakening
A *1:* 122; *2:* 304, 307, 315-18
B *1:* 94-95, 97-98; *2:* 230-31, 241, 356

The Great Christian Doctrine of Original Sin Defended
B *1:* 99

Great Migration
A *1:* 96, 127
B *1:* 20, 109-10
PS 222

Greene, Henry
B *1:* 142

Greene, Thomas
B *1:* 34

Green, Joseph
A *2:* 361

Greenland
A *1:* 12-13
PS 12

Greenwood, Issac
A *2:* 385

Greenwood, John
B *2:* 308

Grenville, Richard
A *1:* 81-82
PS 52-53, 60

Gridley, Jeremiah
PS 290-91

Griffon
A *1:* 72, 74
B *1:* 184

Gristmills
  A *1:* 195, 199
Gronovius, J. F.
  B *1:* 10
Gua, Pierre du
  B *1:* 50
Gulf Stream
  B *1:* 130
  PS 282
Gustavas Vasa
  A *2:* 365
Gustavus I
  B *1:* 116
Guyart, Marie
  B *1:* 133-37

H

Half Moon
  A *1:* 19
  B *1:* 139-41
  PS 5, 5 (ill.)
Half-Way Covenant
  A *1:* 98
  PS 229
Hallam, Lewis
  A *2:* 366
Hamilton, Alexander
  A *1:* 109, 175-76, 176 (ill.)
Hamilton, Andrew
  A *1:* 175
  B *2:* 384, 386-87, 388 (ill.)
  PS 161-64, 163 (ill.), 166-67
Hamilton, George
  B *1:* 38
Hammond, John
  A *2:* 363
Hammon, Jupiter
  A *2:* 363
Harriot, Thomas
  A *1:* 81; *2:* 363, 376
  PS 51-63
Harvard College
  A *2:* 300, 336-39, 337 (ill.)
  PS 286, 288, 290
Harvard, John
  PS 286
Hastings, Elizabeth
  B *2:* 357
Hat Act of 1732
  A *1:* 198
Hawthorne, Nathaniel
  A *1:* 145; *2:* 370

  B *2:* 224
  PS 204
Haynes, John
  A *1:* 96-97
  B *1:* 78
  PS 221, 225
Heaten, John
  A *2:* 344
Heath, Robert
  A *1:* 115
Heckewelder, John
  A *1:* 19
  B *1:* 138, 141
  PS 4
Hennepin, Louis
  A *1:* 73-74; *2:* 354, 379
  B *1:* 186, 191
Henry VIII
  A *1:* 89; *2:* 294-95, 404
  B *2:* 374
  PS 77-78, 78 (ill.)
Henry IV
  A *1:* 64-65
  B *1:* 49-50
**"Here Follows Some Verses
    upon the Burning of
    Our House"**
  PS 247-49
Hesselius, Gustavus
  A *2:* 345
Hiawatha
  A *1:* 22
Higginson, Francis
  B *1:* 109
Hispaniola
  A *1:* 35, 115
  B *1:* 59, 61, 63
  PS 24
Histoire de la Nouvelle-France
  A *2:* 356
*Histoire et description de la Nouvelle
    France*
  A *2:* 356
Historia de la Nuevo-Mexico
  A *2:* 356, 364
*Historical Collections of the Indians
    in New England*
  A *2:* 358
*The History and Present State
    of Virginia*
  A *1:* 203; *2:* 363
  B *1:* 36
  PS 174

History of New England from 1630 to 1649
   B *2:* 371, 377
"The History of the Dividing Line"
   B *1:* 41
Holmes, Oliver Wendall
   B *1:* 28
Hooke, Robert
   B *2:* 207
Hooker, Thomas
   A *1:* 99, 128
   B *1:* 78, 96, 102, 110
   PS 222
Hopewell
   A *1:* 9
Hopi
   A *1:* 10, 15
Horrocks, Elizabeth
   B *1:* 77
Horse racing
   A *2:* 403-05
House of Burgesses
   A *1:* 134, 167, 167 (ill.), 172
   B *1:* 37
   PS 132
"The House of Seven Gables
   A *2:* 370"
Housing, colonial
   A *2:* 227-30, 229 (ill.)
"How the Spaniards Came to Shung-opovi"
   A *1:* 15
Hubbard, Elizabeth Clark
   B *2:* 211
Hubbard, William
   A *2:* 357-58
Hudson, Henry
   A *1:* 102
   B *1:* **138-43**, 138 (ill.)140 (ill.); *2:* 354
   PS 5, 101
Huguenots
   A *1:* 117, 119
Hull, Hannah
   B *2:* 299
Hull, John
   B *2:* 336
Hull, Joseph
   A *1:* 94
Hunter, Robert
   A *2:* 365
Hurons
   A *1:* 21, 24-25, 65-66, 68; *2:* 292, 321

   B *1:* 51-54, 134-35
   PS 40-41, 121
Hutchinson, Anne Marbury
   A *1:* 97-98, 100-01, 151-55, 153 (ill.); *2:* 277-78
   B *1:* 75-76, 88, 106, **144-52**, 144 (ill.), 147 (ill.); *2:* 367, 377
   PS 208-09, 210 (ill.), 211, 213 (ill.), 214-15, 225
Hutchinson, William
   A *1:* 152, 155
   B *1:* 145-46, 150
   PS 208-09, 215

I

Iberville, Pierre Le Moyne sieur d'
   A *1:* 77
Illinois
   PS 47
"Impressions of New Jersey and New York"
   PS 101-16
Incas
   A *1:* 7, 37
   PS 27
Indentured servants
   A *1:* 188, 200-02
   PS 171-72
The Indian Primer
   B *1:* 106
Ingle, Richard
   B *1:* 32
Ingle's Rebellion
   A *1:* 114
   B *1:* 32-33
Inoculation
   B *1:* 131
   PS 282
"In Reference to Her Children"
   PS 245
The Interesting Narrative of the Life of Olaudah Equiano
   B *1:* 114
   PS 183, 188
Inuits
   A *1:* 10, 12, 72
   B *1:* 167
Ipswich
   A *2:* 211
Iron Act of 1750
   A *1:* 198

Iroquois
   A *1:* 2, 23-24, 59, 61, 65-66,
      105; *2:* 257, 262, 292, 321-22
   B *1:* 38, 44-46, 51-53, 135, 185;
      2: 345
   PS 40-41, 105, 108
Iroquois Confederacy
   A *1:* 22; *2:* 324
   B *1:* 84
Isabella
   A *1:* 32-33, 35-36
   B *1:* 60, 64-65
   PS 17, 17 (ill.), 23-24

J

James, Elizabeth Burnell
   B *2:* 361
James I
   A *1:* 84, 87, 89, 112, 166; *2:* 404
   B *1:* 22, 195; *2:* 258, 264, 314,
      316, 373-74, 285, 288
   PS 66, 74, 78
James II
   A *1:* 98, 115, 169
   B *2:* 248, 333
   PS 229
Jamestown Colony
   A *1:* 16, 67, 80, 84-88, 92, 133,
      136, 165-66, 172, 192, 199;
      2: 217, 219-20, 261, 263, 322
   B *1:* 1-2, 4-5, 54, 102; *2:* 258,
      261-63, 265, 278-79, 282-83,
      285, 287, 289, 309, 312-15
   PS 52, 66-67, 71-72, 75, 77, 81,
      131, 134-35, 140
Jefferson, Thomas
   B *1:* 12, 41
   PS 296
Jeffreys, Herbert
   A *1:* 138
   B *1:* 7
   PS 142
Jesuits
   A *1:* 68, 69 (ill.); *2:* 260, 290,
      292, 292 (ill.), 320-21, 328,
      354, 356
   B *1:* 134, 174-75, 177, 177 (ill.);
      2: 340-42, 343 (ill.), 345
   PS 40-41
Jeune, Paul Le
   PS 41

Jogues, Isaac
   B *2:* 341
   PS 108
Johnson, Anthony
   A *2:* 234
   B **1: 153-60;** *2:* 380
Johnson, Edward
   A *2:* 357
Johnson, John
   B *1:* 159
Johnson, Mary
   B *1:* 155-56
Johnson, Richard
   B *1:* 159
Johnson, Samuel
   A *2:* 249
Johnson, Thomas
   A *2:* 347
Johnson, William
   B *1:* 86
Johnston, Henrietta
   A *2:* 345
John Ward House
   A *2:* 370
John Winthrop's Christian
   Experience
   PS 219-30
"Jolliet and Marquette Travel
   the Mississippi"
   PS 39-49
Jolliet, Louis
   A *1:* 68, 71 (ill.), 74; *2:* 322,
      328, 379
   B **1: 161-68,** 162 (ill.), 164 (ill.),
      185, 187
   PS 42-43, 42 (ill.), 47-48
The Journal of Madame Knight
   B *1:* 179
   PS 253-60
"A Journey from Patapsco
   to Annapolis"
   A *2:* 364
Judaism
   A *2:* 311
Jumano
   A *1:* 40
   B *1:* 122

K

Kalm, Per (Peter)
   PS 101-16

Karlsefni
  A *1:* 12
Kean, Thomas
  A *2:* 365
Keith, George
  A *2:* 314
  PS 279
Kepler, Johannes
  A *2:* 383, 384 (ill.), 386
Key into the Language of America
  B *2:* 369
The Keys of the Kingdom of Heaven
  B *1:* 79
Kidd, William
  B *1:* **169-73**, 169 (ill.)
King Charles II
  B *1:* 111
King George III
  B *1:* 11
King James I
  B *1:* 77
King Philip (See Metacom)
King Philip's War (Metacom's
    War)
  A *1:* 130-33, 131 (ill.), 168;
    2: 323
  B *1:* 101; *2:* 204, 217 (ill.), 218,
    290, 294-95, 369
  PS 123, 128, 130-31, 232,
    237 (ill.)
King, Robert
  B *1:* 113, 116
King's College
  A *2:* 339
  PS 288
Kino, Eusebio Francisco
  A *1:* 52-53; *2:* 320, 379
  B *1:* **174-78**
Kitomaquund, Mary
  B *1:* 32
Kneller, Godfrey
  B *2:* 306
Knight, Sarah Kemble
  A *2:* 281
  B *1:* **179-83**, 181 (ill.)
  PS 253-60
Kraft, Valentine
  B *2:* 226

L

La Florida
  A *2:* 355

La Hontan, Louis-Armand de
    Lom d'Arce de
  A *2:* 356
Land taxes
  A *1:* 182
Lane, Ralph
  A *1:* 81
  PS 53
La Peltrie, Madeleine de
  B *1:* 135
**La Salle, René-Robert
    Cavalier de**
  A *1:* 72, 74-76, 75 (ill.); *2:* 368
  B *1:* **184-91**, 184 (ill.), 189 (ill.)
Las Casas, Bartolomé de
  A *1:* 35
  B *1:* 63-64
  PS 25, 25 (ill.)
Laudonnière, René Goulaine de
  A *1:* 62-63
Laud, William
  A *1:* 97
  B *1:* 22
  PS 224, 244
Laval de Montigny, Francois
  A *2:* 328
Law, John
  A *1:* 76
Lawrence, Goody
  A *2:* 274
Lawson, John
  A *2:* 363
League of Five Nations
  B *1:* 84
League of Six Nations
  B *1:* 84
Lederer, John
  A *2:* 378
Leislerians
  B *1:* 198
Leisler, Jacob
  A *1:* 170-72, 171 (ill.)
  B *1:* **192-98**, 192 (ill.)
  PS 105
Leisler's Rebellion
  A *1:* 170
  B *1:* 196-98
Le Jeune, Paul
  A *2:* 354, 356
Lennardson, Samuel
  A *2:* 283
  B *2:* 294

León , Juan Ponce de
  A *1:* 38
  B *2:* 318
  PS 28
Le pays des Illinois
  A *1:* 162
Lescarbot, Marc
  A *2:* 356
Le Théâtre de Neptune en Nouvelle-France
  A *2:* 364
A Letter From Elizabeth Bacon
  PS 131-43
Lewis and Clark expedition
  B *1:* 12
Lewis, Meriwether
  B *1:* 12
Lewis, Richard
  A *2:* 364
Leyden jar
  B *1:* 128-29
  PS 281
Library Company of Philadelphia
  A *2:* 357
The Life of the Venerable Mother Marie de l'Incarnation
  B *1:* 137
Lightning
  B *1:* 129, 131
  PS 282
Lightning rod
  B *1:* 129, 131
  PS 281, 283
Lincoln, Abraham
  PS 186
Lining, John
  A *2:* 391
Linnaeus, Carolus
  B *1:* 8-10, 9 (ill.), 55, 58
Lituya Bay
  PS 7-8, 11
Livingston, Robert
  B *1:* 171, 193, 193 (ill.); *2:* 350
Livingston, William
  A *2:* 362
Locke, John
  A *1:* 116; *2:* 252, 253 (ill.)
  B *1:* 95
  PS 160
Logan, James
  A *2:* 362, 384-85
  B *1:* 8-9

Louisiana
  A *1:* 162
  PS 47-48
Louis XIV
  A *1:* 74; *2:* 340, 379
  B *1:* 186-87, 195; *2:* 245
  PS 47
Louis XIII
  A *1:* 65
  B *1:* 52
  PS 41
Lutheran Church
  B *2:* 226-27
Lutheranism
  A *2:* 308-09, 315
Luther, Martin
  A *1:* 89; *2:* 298, 308, 316
  B *1:* 14; *2:* 227
  PS 78

M

Machiavelli, Niccolò
  B *2:* 310
Magnalia Christi Americana
  A *2:* 358
Maine
  A *1:* 170
Makemie, Francis
  A *2:* 305, 305 (ill.)
Mallet, Paul
  A *2:* 379
Mallet, Pierre
  A *2:* 379
Manteo
  A *1:* 80
  PS 52
A Map of Virginia,
  A *2:* 377
Marcus Aurelius
  B *2:* 310
Marquette, Jacques
  A *1:* 71 (ill.), 73-74; *2:* 322, 354, 379
  B *1:* **161-68**, 162 (ill.), 164 (ill.), 185, 187
  PS **39-49**, 42 (ill.), 45 (ill.)
Martin, Claude
  B *1:* 134
Maryland
  A *1:* 109, 113, 164, 184, 189, 192; *2:* 233, 237, 266, 280, 294 (ill.), 336, 341

Mary II
  A *1:* 98, 114, 170, 184; *2:* 293
  B *2:* 248
  PS 229
Mashantucket Pequot Museum
    and Research Center
  A *1:* 20-21
Maskoutens
  PS 44
Mason, George
  A *1:* 135
  B *1:* 3
  PS 133
Massachusetts
  A *1:* 100-02, 164-65, 168, 170,
    172, 182, 196, 203, 209;
    2: 212, 217, 220, 277,
    281-82, 323, 334
Massachusetts Bay Colony
  A *1:* 93-97, 99, 130, 142-43,
    145, 147, 149, 151-52, 154,
    191, 193, 195; *2:* 220,
    298, 301
  B *1:* 17, 20, 75, 88, 107-08,
    110-11, 144-46, 148, 150-51,
    171; *2:* 208, 214, 219-20,
    222-23, 336, 363, 371, 377
  PS 86-87, 121, 123, 147, 156,
    193-94, 199, 201, 203-04,
    207-09, 211, 219, 221,
    224-25, 230
Massachusetts Bay Company
  B *1:* 23-24; *2:* 371, 374-75
  PS 194, 242, 244
Massasoit
  A *1:* 129
  B *1:* 16, 18; *2:* **199-05**, 199 (ill.),
    201 (ill.), 213, 215-16, 218,
    291, 323, 325-27, 367, 369
  PS 86-87, 123, 233
Mather-Cheever Account of the
    Salem Witch Trials
  PS 145-58
Mather, Cotton
  A *1:* 140, 147, 149; *2:* 224, 341,
    385, 390, 392, 358, 360-62
  B *1:* 37, 41, 102; *2:* **206-12,**
    206 (ill.), 302, 335-36
  PS **145-58,** 151 (ill.), 297
Mather, Increase
  A *1:* 149; *2:* 357-58, 385
  B *2:* 207, 300, 302, 336
  PS 147, 148 (ill.), 156

Mather, Maria Cotton
  B *2:* 207
Mather, Richard
  B *2:* 207
Mayan temple
  A *1:* 8 (ill.)
Mayas
  A *1:* 7, 37
  PS 28
May Day
  A *1:* 93, 142-43, 144 (ill.)
  B *2:* 221 (ill.)
  PS 199-201
Mayflower
  A *1:* 90-91, 90 (ill.), 94; *2:* 219
  B *1:* 15-16, 18
  PS 79-80, 83 (ill.)
Mayflower Compact
  A *1:* 91
  B *1:* 13, 15
  PS 80, 87, 193
Mayhew, Thomas
  A *2:* 323
  B *1:* 102
"The Maypole of
    Merry-Mount"
  PS **193-205**
Meat Out of the Eater
  A *2:* 360
  B *2:* 337
Medicine
  A *2:* 389-91
Megapolensis, Johannes
  A *2:* 322
Melyen, Abigail
  B *2:* 303
Mendenhall, Ann
  B *1:* 9
Mendoza, Antonio de
  A *1:* 40, 47, 49
  B *1:* 68, 73, 123-24
Menéndez de Avilés, Pedro
  A *1:* 44-45, 63, 115, 159, 159
    (ill.)
  B *2:* 319
  PS 29, 37
Men's Musical Society
  A *2:* 353
Merry Mount
  PS 201
Metacom
  A *1:* 23, 129-32, 129 (ill.);
    2: 302

B *1:* 105; *2:* 204, **213-18**, 213 (ill.), 291, 293, 296, 369
PS 123-24, 127 (ill.), 128-30, 233-34, 238

Metacom's War
A *1:* 23, 29; *2:* 302

Methodists
B *2:* 357

Miamis
A *1:* 24
B *2:* 268
PS 44

Michaelius, Jonas
A *2:* 322

Micmacs
A *1:* 12

Milborne, Jacob
A *1:* 171-72

Miller, Arthur
PS 157

Miller, Joan
A *2:* 274

Milton, John
PS 160

Missions
A *2:* 327 (ill.)
B *1:* 138 (ill.)
PS 35 (ill.)

Missisaugas
B *2:* 268

Mitchell, John
A *2:* 389
B *1:* 10

"A Modell of Christian Charity"
B *2:* 375-76
PS 230

Mohawks
A *1:* 22-23,104, 131; *2:* 322, 324
B *2:* 217, 342-43
PS 103, 128

Mohegans
B *1:* 18, 102
PS 86

Mohicans
A *1:* 104
PS 103

Montague, Elizabeth
A *2:* 274

Montauks
A *2:* 324

Montcalm, Louis Joseph de
A *1:* 78

Montezuma
PS 27

Montreal
A *2:* 215

Monts, Pierre du Gua, sieur de
A *1:* 63

Moraley, William
A *2:* 401

Moravian Church
B *2:* 226

Moravians
A *2:* 315

More, Samuel
A *2:* 349

Moros y Cristianos
A *2:* 364

Morrice, William
B *1:* 111

Morris, Lewis
B *2:* 385
PS 160

Morris, Mary
B *1:* 9

Morton, Charles
A *2:* 385

Morton, Nathaniel
A *2:* 357

Morton, Thomas
A *1:* 142-43, 145
B *1:* 109; *2:* **219-24**, 219 (ill.)
PS **193-205**, 203 (ill.), 225

Mühlenberg, Henry Melchior
A *2:* 309, 310 (ill.)
B *2:* **225-29**, 225 (ill.)

Mumford, Ann
B *1:* 103

Munday, Richard
A *2:* 373

Murray, Walter
A *2:* 365

Musgrove, Robert
A *1:* 122

Music
A *2:* 350-54

N

Nanboa, Pedro Don
B *2:* 276

Narragansetts
A *1:* 92, 101,130-31, 128
B *1:* 17-18, 110; *2:* 203-04, 215-16, 218, 324, 328
PS 86, 124, 128, 222

"A Narrative of Bacon's
  Rebellion by William
  Sherwood"
  PS 131-43
*The Narrative of the Captivity
  and Restauration of Mrs.
  Mary Rowlandson*
  PS 231-40
*A Narrative of the Troubles with the
  Indians in New-England*
  A *2:* 357
Narváez, Pánfilo de
  B *1:* 120
Native Americans
  A *1:* 21 (ill.)
  PS 10 (ill.)
*The Naturall and Morall Historie of
  the East and West Indie*
  A *2:* 375
Naumkeag
  A *1:* 94
Navigation Act of 1651
  A *1:* 169, 193
Neale, John
  B *1:* 157
Neff, Mary
  A *2:* 282
  B *2:* 294
Neo-Palladian architecture
  A *2:* 372
New Amsterdam
  A *1:* 103, 103 (ill.), 105; *2:* 212,
    276, 322
  B *2:* 329, 331-32, 351
  PS 103-06, 108, 115
New England
  A *1:* 94, 100-02
New England Company
  A *1:* 94-95
  B *1:* 31
  PS 220
New England Confederation
  A *1:* 168
The New England Primer
  A *2:* 329-31, 330 (ill.)
New Englands Memoriall
  A *2:* 357
New English Canaan
  A *1:* 145
  B *2:* 220, 222-23
  PS 200, 203-04
New France
  A *1:* 64, 66, 68, 72, 157; *2:* 354

B *1:* 48, 53, 161, 163, 184
  PS 41
New Galicia
  A *1:* 50
  B *1:* 68, 73
  PS 28
New Hampshire
  A *2:* 212, 324
New Haven, Connecticut
  A *1:* 100; *2:* 339
New Jersey
  A *1:* 164, 189, 191; *2:* 212, 277
New Netherland
  A *1:* 155, 170; *2:* 237, 269, 275,
    322, 324-25, 328-29, 340
  B *1:* 138, 150, 192, 194; *2:* 329,
    332
  PS 215
New Orleans, Louisiana
  A *2:* 215
Newport, Christopher
  A *1:* 84-85
  B *2:* 312-13
  PS 66-67
Newport Parish Church
  A *2:* 372
Newport, Rhode Island
  A *1:* 101
New Spain
  A *1:* 159
Newspapers
  A *1:* 209-10
Newton, Issac
  A *2:* 383-86
  B *1:* 95; *2:* 210, 255
A New Voyage to Carolina
  A *2:* 363
New York
  A *1:* 164, 172, 181, 184, 189,
    191, 206, 209; *2:* 212
New York City
  A *2:* 339
New York Gazette
  B *2:* 385
New-York Weekly Journal
  A *1:* 175
  B *2:* 384-86, 389
  PS 160, 166
Niantics
  A *1:* 20
Nicholson, Francis
  B *1:* 196

Nicolet, Jean
  A *1:* 67-68
  B *1:* 53-54
Nicolls, Richard
  A *2:* 404
Niña
  A *1:* 32
  B *1:* 60
  PS 17
Nipissing
  B *1:* 54
Nipmucks
  A *1:* 130-31
  B *2:* 215-16
  PS 123, 128
Niza, Marcos de
  A *1:* 46-48
  B *1:* 69-70, 72, 122-24
Nonconformists
  B *1:* 14, 18
North Carolina
  A *1:* 115-16, 118-19; *2:* 214
Northwest Passage
  A *1:* 56, 58
"Nouveaux Voyages"
  A *2:* 356
Nuestra Señiora de la Purisima
      Concepción de Acuna
  A *2:* 366
Nuthead, Dinah
  A *2:* 280

O

Ocaneechee
  A *1:* 136
  B *1:* 4
  PS 135
Occom, Samson
  A *2:* 324
  B *2:* 230-36, **230 (ill.)**
Of Plymouth Plantation
  A *1:* 143; *2:* 358
  B *1:* 13, 17, 20; *2:* 220
  PS 81, 200
Oglethorpe, James Edward
  A *1:* 18 (ill.), 119-23; *2:* 364
  B *2:* **237-43**, 237 (ill.),
      242 (ill.), 359
Ohio Company
  A *1:* 78
Ojeda, Alonso de
  A *1:* 35

  B *1:* 62
  PS 26
Ojlbwas
  A *1:* 24
  B *2:* 268, 270
Oldham, John
  A *1:* 128
  B *1:* 110-11
  PS 223
Old North Church
  A *2:* 373
Old Ship Meeting House
  A *2:* 370
Old South Church
  A *2:* 373
Olmecs
  A *1:* 7
Oñate, Juan de
  B *2:* 274
One Hundred Associates
  A *1:* 66
  B *1:* 53
Oneidas
  A *1:* 21-22
  B *1:* 84
Onondagas
  A *1:* 21-22
  B *1:* 84
Oort, Sarah
  B *1:* 170
Otertmín, Antonio de
  B *2:* 276
Otis, James
  PS 290
Ottawas
  A *1:* 24
  B *2:* 267-68, 270
Ovando, Nicolas de
  B *1:* 66

P

Padilla, Juan de
  A *1:* 48
  B *1:* 72
Paleo-Indian Period
  A *1:* 5-6
Paleo-Indians
  A *1:* 5
Palladio, Andrea
  A *2:* 372
Parke, Daniel
  B *1:* 37

Parke, Lucy
  B *1:* 37
Parker, Robert
  B *1:* 157
"A Parody on a Hymn by
    Mather Byles"
  A *2:* 361
Parson Capen House
  A *2:* 370
Particular Baptists
  A *2:* 307
Pascal, Michael Henry
  B *1:* 113, 115
Pastorius, Francis
  A *1:* 140
  PS 184
Pattison, Jane
  A *2:* 274
Patuxet
  B *2:* 323-24
Pawmunkey
  A *1:* 137
  B *1:* 5
  PS 136
Peale, Charles Willson
  A *2:* 347
Pelham, Peter
  A *2:* 347
Pemberton, Hannah
  A *2:* 380
Pennsylvania
  A *1:* 109, 112, 164, 172, 180,
    182-83, 188-89, 191, 193,
    196, 200-01; *2:* 212, 241,
    277, 280, 335, 339, 341
Pennsylvania Council
  B *1:* 82
Pennsylvania fireplace
  B *1:* 131
  PS 283
Pennsylvania Ministerium
  B *2:* 225
Penn, William
  A *1:* 106-08, 107 (ill.), 115,
    188; *2:* 212, 277, 313-14,
    361-62, 406
  B *1:* 31, 84; *2:* **244-50**, 246 (ill.)
  PS **89-100**, 90 (ill.), 91 (ill.),
    96 (ill.)
The People
  B *1:* 73
Pequots
  A *1:* 20, 92, 96, 128

  B *1:* 17-18, 110-11, 190
  PS 86, 222-23
Pequot War
  A *1:* 21, 92, 127, 127 (ill.),
    129, 153
  B *1:* 17-18, 90, 107, 110-11,
    148; *2:* 215
  PS 86, 131, 211, 223 (ill.), 224
Perry, Joseph
  A *2:* 252
Petuns
  A *1:* 24-25
Philadelphia Assembly
  A *2:* 353
Philadelphia, Pennsylvania
  A *1:* 117; *2:* 341
  PS 279 (ill.)
Phillips, Abigail
  B *2:* 208
Phillips, Wendall
  B *1:* 28
Pictograph
  A *1:* 3 (ill.)
Pilgrims
  A *1:* 95; *2:* 218
  B *1:* 13, 15, 15 (ill.); *2:* 323
  PS 81, 85, 194, 194, (ill.),
    204, 219
**"The Pilgrims' Landing and
    First Winter"**
  PS *77-88*, 194
Pimas
  A *1:* 52
  B *1:* 175
Pinckney, Eliza Lucas
  A *2:* 280, 380
  B *2:* **251-56**, 255 (ill.)
Pinta
  A *1:* 32
  B *1:* 60
  PS 17
Pizarro, Francisco
  A *1:* 41
  B *1:* 69; *2:* 318
  PS 27
Plantations
  A *1:* 192, 199
"The Pleasures of a Country Life"
  PS 251
Plymouth
  A *1:* 84, 93-94, 101, 116, 130,
    142-43, 145, 165-66, 170,

172; *2:* 211, 217, 219-20, 298, 301
   B *2:* 200, 202-03, 316
Plymouth Colony
   A *1:* 65, 91-92, 95; *2:* 378
   B *1:* 13, 19-20, 50; *2:* 200, 203, 214, 323, 325, 327-28
   PS 65, 75, 80-81, 87, 121-23, 193-94, 199-200, 202-04, 219-20
Plymouth Company
   B *1:* 108
Plymouth Council
   B *1:* 108
Plymouth Rock
   A *1:* 91
   B *1:* 16
   PS 80
Pocahontas
   A *1:* 87; *2:* 218, 261, 261 (ill.)
   B *1:* 102; *2:* 257-65, 257 (ill.), 258 (ill.), 281-83, 286-87, 288 (ill.), 309, 314
   PS 73-74
"Poème en vers"
   A *2:* 356
Poetical Meditations
   A *2:* 361
   B *2:* 335
Pokanokets
   B *2:* 323
Poll tax
   A *1:* 182
Pontiac
   B *2:* **266-72**, 266 (ill.), 268 (ill.)
Pontiac's Rebellion
   B *2:* 266
Poor Richard's Almanack
   A *2:* 386-87, 386 (ill.)
   B *1:* 126
   PS 272
Popé
   A *1:* 51; *2:* 291
   B *2:* **273-77**
   PS 37-38, 121
Portrait painting
   A *2:* 344
Port Royal Sound
   A *1:* 115-16
Portsmouth, Rhode Island
   A *1:* 101
Postal service
   A *1:* 208-09, 208 (ill.)

Postmasters
   A *1:* 209
Potawatomis
   A *1:* 24
Potawototi
   B *1:* 185
Poverty Point
   A *1:* 9
Powhatan
   A *1:* 85-87; *2:* 218, 261
   B *1:* 102; *2:* 257, 63-64, **278-82**, 278 (ill.), 280 (ill.), 286-87, 309, 314
   PS 66, 66 (ill.), 71-74
Powhatan Confederacy
   A *1:* 16
Powhatans
   A *1:* 84, 86-87, 199; *2:* 219, 323, 376
   B *2:* 257-58, 260, 263, 278-79, 283, 286-89, 313-14
   PS 66, 72, 74, 121
Presbyterianism
   A *2:* 304-07, 310, 318
Presbyterians
   B *2:* 373
   PS 222
Price, William
   A *2:* 373
Priestman, Thomas
   B *2:* 382
The Prince of Parthia
   A *2:* 366
Prince, Thomas
   A *2:* 358
Princeton College
   A *2:* 306, 339
   PS 288
Princeton, New Jersey
   A *2:* 339
Printers
   A *1:* 209
The Propriety of Pennsylvania
   PS 89-100
Protestant Reformation
   A *2:* 308
Providence, Rhode Island
   A *1:* 101
Pueblo
   A *1:* 11 (ill.)
Pueblo Bonito
   A *1:* 10
Pueblo Revolt
   A *1:* 160

Pueblos
  A *1:* 40, 50-51; *2:* 290-91, 320
  B *1:* 121-22; *2:* 273-77
  PS 30-32, 36, 121
Punishment, colonial
  A *1:* 179 (ill.); *2:* 248 (ill.)
Puritanism
  A *2:* 293, 304, 309-10
Puritans
  A *1:* 21 (ill.), 96-101, 129,
    143, 145, 150-52; *2:* 225 (ill.),
    240, 249, 269, 270 (ill.), 271,
    273, 276, 278, 298-302, 323,
    337, 339
  B *1:* 76, 79, 88-90, 101-02, 107,
    110, 144-45; *2:* 206, 209,
    219-20, 222, 224, 291, 298-
    99, 335-36, 339, 363-64, 369,
    371, 374-75
  PS 193-99, 194 (ill.), 204,
    207-09, 211, 219-21, 224-26,
    229, 232, 243
Putnam, James
  PS 290

Q

Quakerism
  B *2:* 244-45, 247
Quakers
  A *1:* 101, 112, 114, 119, 141,
    158, 174; *2:* 212, 241, 244,
    277, 312, 313 (ill.), 314-15,
    339, 341
  B *1:* 9, 88, 90, 92, 109,
    111, 116-17; *2:* 368-69,
    378-80, 382
  PS 185, 216, 261-64, 265 (ill.)
Quanopin
  B *2:* 293
Quapaws
  A *1:* 70
  B *1:* 164
  PS 43
Quebec
  A *1:* 67 (ill.); *2:* 215
Quincy, Edmund
  B *1:* 78
Quitrents
  A *1:* 182
Qunnipiacs
  A *1:* 28

R

Rackham, Calico Jack
  B *1:* 172
Raleigh, Walter
  A *1:* 80-81, 80 (ill.), 115; *2:* 376
  B *1:* 26
  PS 52, 53 (ill.), 60
Read, Mary
  B *1:* 172
Redemptioners
  A *1:* 201
Reed, Deborah
  B *1:* 132
  PS 283
A Relaction of the Indyan Warre
  PS 119-30
Rensselaerswyck
  B *2:* 348
Revolutionary War
  B *2:* 255
Rhode Island
  A *1:* 100-01, 164, 184, 203,
    209; *2:* 212, 334
  B *2:* 215
Ribault, Jean
  A *1:* 45, 62-63, 115
Richelieu, Armand Jean du
    Plessis, duc de
  A *1:* 66
  B *1:* 53
Right Thoughts in Sad Hours
  A *2:* 360
  B *2:* 335
Roanokes
  A *1:* 80-81
  PS 52-53
Roanoke, Virginia
  A *1:* 80-82, 83 (ill.); *2:* 376
  PS 52-54, 57 (ill.), 60-63
Roberval, Jean-François de La
    Rocque
  A *1:* 60, 62
  B *1:* 46, 47
Robie, Thomas
  A *2:* 385
Robinson, John
  A *2:* 244
Robinson, William
  B *1:* 90, 111
Rogueneau, Paul
  A *2:* 321, 354
Rolfe, John
  A *1:* 87, 192; *2:* 261

B *2:* 263-65, 282, **283-89,**
283 (ill.), 288 (ill.)
PS 74, 169, 170 (ill.)
Roman Catholic Church
B *2:* 227
Roman Catholic Inquisition
B *1:* 194
Roman Catholicism
A *1:* 32, 51, 68, 114, 160;
2: 291-92
B *1:* 30, 31, 33, 110, 133, 174;
2: 273
PS 16, 30, 32, 34, 37, 39-40
Rosier, James
A *2:* 377
Rowlandson, Joseph
B *2:* 291
PS 232, 234
Rowlandson, Mary White
A *2:* 283, 283 (ill.)
B *2:* **290-97,** 290 (ill.), 292 (ill.)
PS **231-40,** 233 (ill.)
Royal Society
B *1:* 37

S

Sacred History
B *1:* 137
"Saga of Erik the Red"
A *1:* 12
PS 12
Sagard, Gabriel
A *2:* 256
Saint Augustine, Florida
A *1:* 14, 45 (ill.); *2:* 234
B *2:* 319
PS 29, 31 (ill.), 39
Salem, Massachusetts
A *1:* 95; *2:* 334
PS 154
Salem witch trials
B *2:* 300 (ill.)
PS 153 (ill.), 155, 167
San Diego de Alcala Mission
B *1:* 136 (ill.)
Sandwith, Elizabeth
A *2:* 269
Sandys, Edwin
B *1:* 158
Santa Elena
A *1:* 115

Santa Maria
A *1:* 32
B *1:* 60, 62
PS 17
Sassamon, John
A *1:* 130
PS 124
Sauks
A *1:* 24
Savannah, Georgia
A *1:* 121 (ill.), 122
Sawmills
A *1:* 195
Saybrook platform
A *2:* 303
Scarlet Letter Law
A *2:* 273
Schlatter, Michael
A *2:* 312
Schools
A *2:* 334-36, 335 (ill.), 351
The Secret History of the Line
A *2:* 363
B *1:* 41
The Selling of Joseph
A *1:* 140
B *2:* 303
PS 185
Selyns, Henricus
A *2:* 362
Seminoles
A *1:* 17-18
Senecas
A *1:* 21-22
B *1:* 81, 83-84; *2:* 268, 270
Separatists
B *1:* 109; *2:* 373
"Servants and Slaves
in Virginia"
PS **69-80,** 184
Seven Cities of Cíbola
A *1:* 40, 46
B *1:* 68-70; 119, 122-24
PS 28
Seven Years' War
A *1:* 173
B *1:* 113
Sewall, Samuel
A *1:* 140, 149-50; *2:* 244,
248, 385
B *2:* **298-04,** 298 (ill.) 307
PS **145-58,** 184
Shawnees
A *1:* 17, 23-24; *2:* 323
B *1:* 86; *2:* 268, 271

Shenandoah Valley
  A *1:* 119
Sherwood, William
  PS 131-43
Shipbuilding
  A *1:* 193, 194 (ill.), 199, 205
Shippen, Edward
  B *1:* 82
Sibbes, Richard
  B *1:* 77
Silk winding
  B *2:* 255 (ill.)
Sille, Nicasius de
  A *2:* 362
The Simple Cobbler of Aggawam in America
  A *2:* 360
"Sinners in the Hands of an Angry God"
  A *2:* 317
  B *1:* 94, 97-98
Sioux
  A *1:* 24
Skillin, Samuel
  A *2:* 350
Slave laborers
  A *1:* 139-41, 200, 202, 204
Slave quarters
  A *2:* 235 (ill.)
Slavery
  B *1:* 115 (ill.), 156 (ill.); *2:* 380, 382
  PS 183-86, 191
Slaves
  PS 172, 174, 176 (ill.), 182 (ill.)
Slave trade
  A *1:* 138-39, 139 (ill.), 141, 174, 188, 192, 203-04, 205 (ill.), 255 (ill.)
  PS 181-83, 185
Sloane, Hans
  B *1:* 10
Sloughter, Henry
  A *1:* 171
  B *1:* 197-98
Sluyter, Peter
  A *2:* 338
  PS 288
Smallpox inoculation
  B *2:* 211
Smibert, John
  A *1:* 85 (ill.); *2:* 345, 347
  B *2:* **305-08**, 305 (ill.)

Smith, Elizabeth Murray
  A *2:* 279
Smith, John
  A *1:* 85, 87; *2:* 218, 261-62, 377-78, 397
  B *1:* 54, 139; *2:* 257, 258 (ill.), 262, 279, 284, 286, **309-16**, 309 (ill.), 315 (ill.)
  PS **65-76**, 70 (ill.)
Smith, William
  PS 161
Society for the Propagation of the Gospel in Foreign Parts
  A *1:* 140; *2:* 341
  PS 184
Society of Friends
  A *1:* 141
  PS 185, 190, 222
Some Account of the Early Part of the Life of Elizabeth Ashbridge, . . . Written by Herself
  PS 261-69
Some Considerations on the Keeping of Negroes
  A *1:* 141, 174
  PS **181-92**
Soto, Hernando de
  A *1:* 41-43, 41 (ill.), 43 (ill.), 115; *2:* 355
  B *2:* **317-22**, 317 (ill.), 321 (ill.)
  PS 28, 43
The Sot-Weed Factor
  A *2:* 364
South Carolina
  A *1:* 115, 118; *2:* 214, 233-34, 265, 280, 336, 341
Southwell, Robert
  B *1:* 37
Southworth, Alice Carpenter
  B *1:* 16
Sower, Christopher
  A *2:* 316
Spanish
  A *1:* 158, 160
Spencer, Archibald
  A *2:* 388
Spiritual Milk for Boston Babes in Either England
  B *1:* 79, 79 (ill.)
Spotswood, Alexander
  B *1:* 35, 38-39, 38 (ill.)
"Spurring-Verses"
  A *2:* 361

Squanto
  A *1:* 92; *2:* 219, 220 (ill.)
  B *2:* 200-02, **323-28**, 323 (ill.),
    326 (ill.)
  PS 81, 84
Stamp Act
  A *1:* 182
Standish, Miles
  A *1:* 91, 143, 172
  B *1:* 16, 18-19; *2:* 222
  PS 80, 84, 203
Stanley Whitman House
  A *2:* 370
Static electricity
  B *1:* 128
  PS 281
Steele, Richard
  A *2:* 366
Steendam, Jacob
  A *2:* 361
Steere, Richard
  A *2:* 362
Stephenson, Marmaduke
  B *1:* 90, 111
St. Mark's Episcopal Church
  B *2:* 334
Stoddard, Solomon
  A *2:* 303-04
  B *1:* 95-97
Stone, John
  A *1:* 128
  B *1:* 110
  PS 223
Strachey, William
  A *2:* 377
  B *2:* 260
Stratford Hall
  A *2:* 372
Stuyvesant, Peter
  A *1:* 104, 163, 163 (ill.); *2:* 237,
    329, 340
  B *2:* **329-34**, 329 (ill.), 351, 385
  PS 104, 105 (ill.), 115
"Stuyvesant's Bad Government"
  B *2:* 331
Sugar Act
  A *1:* 182
Sulpicians
  B *1:* 185
Susquehannocks
  A *1:* 24, 135
  B *1:* 3
  PS 133

T

Tadodahoh
  A *1:* 22
Tailfer, Patrick
  A *2:* 363
Tainos
  B *1:* 61
  PS 17
Taney, Mary
  A *2:* 279
Taylor, Edward
  A *2:* 360
  B *2:* **335-39**
  PS 243
Tea Act
  A *1:* 182
Tea parties
  A *2:* 399 (ill.)
Tekakwitha, Catherine (Kateri)
  B *2:* **340-46**, 340 (ill.)
  PS 121 (ill.)
Temple, Thomas
  B *1:* 91
Tenant farmers
  A *1:* 189
Tennent, Gilbert
  A *2:* 306
  B *2:* 361, 361 (ill.)
Tennent, William
  A *2:* 306
Tenochtitlán
  A *1:* 8
*The Tenth Muse Lately Sprung Up in
    America*
  A *2:* 282, 282 (ill.),
    359 (ill.), 360
  B *1:* 21, 24, 25 (ill.), 26
  PS 245 (ill.), 246-47
Texcoco
  A *1:* 8
Textile manufacturing
  A *1:* 195
Thanksgiving
  A *1:* 93 (ill.)
  B *1:* 17; *2:* 202
Theüs, Jeremiah
  A *2:* 345
They Came From the East
  A *1:* 37
  PS 28
Thirty Years War
  B *1:* 194
Tidewater
  B *1:* 155

"Tiguex War"
  A *1:* 48
  B *1:* 72
Timothy, Elizabeth
  A *2:* 280
Tlacopán
  A *1:* 8
Tlingits
  PS 6
Tobacco
  A *1:* 192; *2:* 216, 230
Tobacco, harvesting of
  A *1:* 111 (ill.)
Tobacco plantation
  B *2:* 284 (ill.)
Tolerance Act
  B *2:* 247
Toltecs
  A *1:* 7
**"To My Dear and Loving
  Husband"**
  PS 247
Tonti, Henry de
  A *1:* 73
  B *1:* 186-87, 190
Tostee, Peter
  B *1:* 82
Tovar, Pedro de
  A *1:* 48
  B *1:* 72
Toys, colonial
  A *2:* 246 (ill.)
Trading post
  PS 102 (ill.)
Treatise on Religious Affections
  B *1:* 97
Treaty of Fontainebleau
  A *1:* 162
Treaty of Hartford
  A *1:* 129
  B *1:* 110
  PS 224
Trenchard, John
  PS 160
Trinity
  A *1:* 44
Trinity Church
  A *2:* 373
*A True and Historical Narrative of
  the Colony of Georgia*
  A *2:* 363
Trumbull, John
  B *2:* 308

The Tuesday Club
  A *2:* 354
Turner House
  A *2:* 370
Tuscaroras
  A *1:* 24
  B *1:* 84
Twightwees
  B *1:* 84-85
Tyler, Maria
  B *1:* 39
Tyndal, Margaret
  B *2:* 372
  PS 220

U

Uncas
  B *2:* 230-31
United States Constitution
  PS 166
United States Geological Survey
  B *1:* 12
"Upon a Spider Catching a Fly"
  B *2:* 337, 339
"Upon Wedlock & Death of
  Children"
  B *2:* 335, 337

V

Van Cortlandt, Stephanus
  B *2:* 349
Van der Donck, Adriaen
  A *2:* 361
Vanderlyn, Pieter
  A *2:* 344
Vane, Henry
  A *1:* 97, 98 (ill.)
  PS 225
Van Rensselaer, Jeremias
  B *2:* 348, 350
Van Rensselaer, Kiliaen
  A *1:* 104
  B *2:* 348, 350
  PS 103-04, 104 (ill.)
**Van Rensselaer, Maria van
  Cortlandt**
  A *2:* 276
  B *2:* 347-50
  PS 269
Van Rensselaer, Nicholas
  B *1:* 194; *2:* 349

Vega, Garcilaso de la
  A *2:* 355
Vérendrye, Sieur de La
  A *2:* 379
Verrazano, Giovanni da
  A *1:* 56-58, 57 (ill.)
  B *1:* 43, 139; *2:* **351-55,** 351
    (ill.)
Verrazano, Girolamo
  A *1:* 56
  B *2:* 352
Villagrá, Gaspar Pérez de
  A *2:* 356, 364
Virginia
  A *1:* 110, 112, 115, 118-19,
    164, 167, 172, 182, 184;
    2: 218, 220, 223, 233, 237,
    239-40, 263, 266, 322, 336,
    338, 341
Virginia Colony
  A *1:* 188, 192, 202
Virginia Company
  B *1:* 15, 31; *2:* 258, 260-61, 264,
    284-85, 288, 312, 316
  PS 169
Virginia Company of London
  A *1:* 88, 112, 165; *2:* 323
  PS 77
Virginia Company of Plymouth
  A *1:* 88
  PS 77
Volta, Alessandro
  B *1:* 128
*Voyages of Samuel de Champlain,
    1604-1618*
  B *1:* 51
Vries, David de
  PS 108

W

Wage laborers
  A *1:* 202
Wampanoags
  A *1:* 22, 92, 129-32; *2:* 323, 302
  B *1:* 16, 18, 105; *2:* 200, 204,
    213, 216-18, 290-91, 294-96,
    325, 367, 369
  PS 81, 86-87, 121-24, 129-30,
    232-35, 238
Wanchese
  A *1:* 80
  PS 52

Ward, Nathaniel
  A *2:* 360
Warnard, Mary
  B *2:* 364
War of Jenkins' Ear
  B *2:* 252
War of Spanish Succession
  A *1:* 120
  B *1:* 170, 172
Warren, Richard
  B *1:* 18
Wars of Religion
  A *1:* 62-63
Warwick Patent
  B *1:* 19
Warwick, Rhode Island
  A *1:* 101
Washington, George
  A *1:* 78, 138; *2:* 239
  B *1:* 7, 11; *2:* 256
  PS 143, 296
Watson, John
  A *2:* 345
Watts, Isaac
  A *2:* 360
Wax modeling
  A *2:* 350
*The Way of the Churches of Christ
    in New England*
  B *1:* 79
Weddings, colonial
  A *2:* 241 (ill.), 271 (ill.)
Weiser, Conrad
  B *1:* 83, 85
Welch, John
  A *2:* 349
Weld, Joseph
  A *1:* 155
  B *1:* 149
  PS 215
Wesley, Charles
  A *1:* 122; *2:* 360
  B *2:* 240, 357
Wesley, John
  A *1:* 122; *2:* 360
  B *2:* 240, 357, 360
West, Benjamin
  A *2:* 347
Westminster Assembly
  A *2:* 305
Weston, Thomas
  A *1:* 94, 116
The Westover Manuscripts

B *1:* 41
Westover plantation
  A *2:* 372
Whales
  A *1:* 196
Wheatley, Phillis
  A *2:* 363
Wheelock, Eleazor
  A *2:* 324, 324 (ill.)
  B *2:* 230, 233-34
Wheelwright, John
  A *1:* 153-54
  B *1:* 148-49
  PS 211
Whipple House
  A *2:* 370
Whitaker, Alexander
  A *2:* 323
Whitefield, George
  A *1:* 122, 206; *2:* 304, 316-18,
    318 (ill.)
  B *1:* 97, 116; *2:* 240, **356-62,**
    356 (ill.)
White, John
  A *1:* 81-82
  B *1:* 108
  PS 53, 60-63
Whytt, Robert
  B *1:* 57
Wigglesworth, Michael
  A *2:* 360
  B *2:* 337
  PS 243
Williamsburg, Virginia
  A *2:* 211, 338
Williams, Eunice
  A *2:* 283
Williams, Hannah
  A *2:* 380
Williams, Roger
  A *1:* 56, 97, 100, 100 (ill.); *2:*
    306
  B *1:* 79, 90; *2:* 215, 247, 351,
    354, **363-70,** 363 (ill.), 366
    (ill.), 377
  PS 225
William III
  A *1:* 98, 108, 114, 184; *2:* 293
  B *1:* 170, 195-98; *2:* 248
  PS 98, 229
Wilson, John
  A *1:* 152; *2:* 358
  B *1:* 89, 92, 103, 148

PS 210
Winnebagos
  A *1:* 24, 68
  B *1:* 54
Winthrop, John
  A *1:* 94-98, 95 (ill.), 100, 154;
    2: 215, 220, 358, 403
  B *1:* 17, 22, 24, 77, 80, 91, 103,
    108, 148; *2:* 223, 299, 364,
    367, **371-77,** 371 (ill.), 379
  PS 211, **219-30,** 227 (ill.), 244
Winthrop Jr., John
  A *2:* 385
Winthrop, Katherine
  B *2:* 303
Winthrop IV, John
  A *2:* 385
Witch trials
  A *1:* 148 (ill.), 150
  B *2:* 301
Wolfe, James
  A *1:* 78
Women, colonial
  A *2:* 264 (ill.)
Women, Native American
  A *2:* 262 (ill.)
Wonders of the Invisible World
  A *1:* 149
  B *2:* 210
  PS 148
Woodbridge, John
  B *1:* 24
  PS 246
Woolen Act of 1699
  A *1:* 198
Woolman, John
  A *1:* 141, 141 (ill.), 174
  B *2:* 302, **378-83,** 378 (ill.)
  PS **181-92,** 185 (ill.)
Wrangel, Karl Gustaf
  B *2:* 228
Wren, Christopher
  A *2:* 373
Wyandots
  B *1:* 83; *2:* 270
Wyllys, Ruth
  B *2:* 336

X

Xila Apaches
  PS 34

Y

Yale College
　A *2:* 339
　PS 287
Yale, Elihu
　A *2:* 339
　PS 287
Yamasee War
　A *1:* 17
Yeamans, John
　A *1:* 118
Yumas
　A *1:* 52
　B *1:* 175

Z

Zenger, Anna
　B *2:* 385-86, 389
　PS 161, 166
Zenger, John Peter
　A *1:* 175-76, 176 (ill.)
　B *2:* 384-89
　PS 160-63, 161 (ill.), 165-66
Zinzendorf, Nikolaus von
　A *2:* 309, 315
　B *2:* 226
Zunis
　A *1:* 46-47
　B *1:* 119, 122, 125